Honey and Toto:
the story of a cheetah family

Jonathan and Angela Scott

 CAMBRIDGE
UNIVERSITY PRESS

 UCL
Institute of Education

Jonathan and Angela Scott's story

Angie and I travel around the world to watch and photograph wild animals. We bring back stories of amazing places and animals we have seen.

We called the mother cheetah 'Honey', because of the golden brown colour of her eyes.

This is the true story of a brave mother cheetah and her family. It tells how she tried to look after her cubs through many dangers. It shows how life in the wild is very hard.

It is a story of the **triumph** of **courage**.

We meet Honey the cheetah

We first saw Honey in the Masai Mara, in Kenya, Africa.
She lived on the wide African **plains** where cheetahs have
many enemies. Cheetahs are the fastest animals on Earth,
but they do not have the strength to fight lions,
or leopards, or even **hyenas**. So, like all cheetahs,
Honey was used to danger.

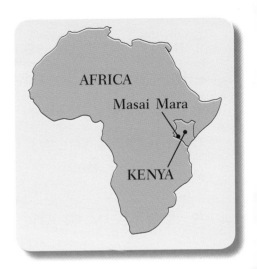

cheetah catching a young gazelle

4

Honey lived on her own for most of the time. She wandered over the grassy plains and woodlands, hunting gazelles and wildebeest and other smaller animals.

Fact Box
Cheetahs can run at 70 miles per hour.

Cheetahs cannot run fast for long. They must catch their **prey** quickly.

Toto is born

Cheetah cubs are usually born on the grassland or light woodland, and are often killed by other animals.

When Honey was about six years old, she gave birth to a cub. We named him Toto. He was the only cub to survive. We don't know what happened to Toto's brothers and sisters. All we know is that Toto was about two months old when we first saw him.

Toto means 'child' in Swahili, the most common language in East Africa.

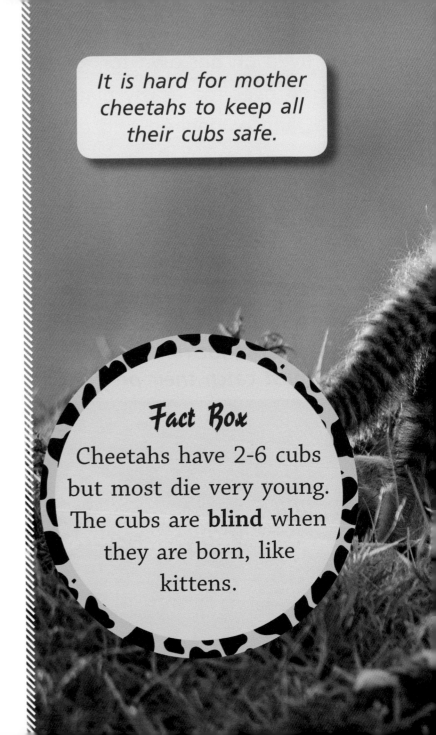

It is hard for mother cheetahs to keep all their cubs safe.

Fact Box
Cheetahs have 2-6 cubs but most die very young. The cubs are **blind** when they are born, like kittens.

Toto was gorgeous. Like all cheetahs, he had black 'tear marks' from his eyes to his mouth. Scientists think that they help cheetahs to see in bright sunlight.

Toto was full of life, but he was very small. Honey was a careful mother, and when she went hunting, she made sure that her cub was well hidden.

Toto likes **exploring**, but it is safer for him to stay hidden.

All cheetah cubs have long grey hair along their backs. This hair helps to hide the cubs in the long grass where they live. Cheetah cubs lose this hair when they are about 3 months old.

long grey hair

Fact Box
Cubs weigh just 85-300 grams when they are born.

Hunting

Honey had to hunt to feed herself and Toto. She had to leave Toto on his own when she was hunting. If other animals found him, they might kill him.

The sight and smell of food attracts other animals, such as lions, vultures and hyenas. They want to steal the food, and that would put Honey and Toto in danger.

Honey did not want to fight a lion or a leopard on her own. If she got hurt, she could not look after Toto. They would both die. It was better to keep moving and hide her little cub away from danger.

Honey is looking out for danger.

Fact Box

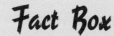

Cheetahs hunt in the daytime. They often hunt in the middle of the day when it is very hot. This is when most animals like to rest in the shade. Cheetahs hunt at this time because they are not strong enough to compete with other big cats.

Large eagles sometimes kill cheetah cubs.

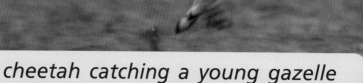

cheetah catching a young gazelle

Toto was a clever cub, and while his mother was hunting, he would hide out of sight. If she caught a gazelle, she would call out to Toto.

Toto learned to recognize her cry. It was a high, yelping sound. He would race towards his mother, making a cheeping sound like a bird. He knew that she had found food for them both.

Toto is learning how to look out for danger. Other animals will have seen the kill.

Then they would eat and Toto would play hunting games. He already wanted to learn how to hunt by himself. Honey would lick Toto's fur clean after he had eaten.

Toto and Honey are playing, but Toto is learning all the time.

Honey is giving Toto a good wash.

When it rains

We watched Toto and Honey nearly every day. The weather was very hot, but sometimes, the sky would fill with black clouds and it would pour with rain.

If it rained, Honey would stand over Toto to keep him warm and dry. Without her, he would have died.

Honey always protected Toto from the rain.

As Toto grew up, Honey had no more milk for him and she had to hunt almost every day. Sometimes, there was no food at all. Then he **whined** because he was hungry. Honey would lick his fur lovingly and he seemed to feel better. She had to work hard to find enough food for them both.

Toto learns from Honey

Toto watched his mother. He was always ready to follow her wherever she went. By the time that Toto was four months old, he could run away from danger. But he needed his mother to warn him when danger was coming. Toto was still very small.

Honey spent hours staring across the plains. She had to be ready for anything. She liked to go as high up as she could. She would choose a small **mound**, so that she could see everything around her.

Fact Box

Cheetahs cannot climb trees well. They must rely on their speed and skill to get out of danger.

Cheetahs can also hear the smallest sound.

Like all cheetahs, Honey has very good eyesight during the day, but she does not see well at night.

Danger!

We were always worried that something would happen to Honey and Toto. One day, Honey killed a gazelle. Then two male baboons headed towards the kill. Would they find Toto? Would he be killed? We held our breath.

But Honey was ready for the baboons.

Baboons can be dangerous and they could have killed Toto.

Honey is always ready for danger. She sees the two baboons before they see Toto.

Honey runs bravely towards the baboons.

She ran towards them, trying to lead them away from her cub. Toto was worried. He knew he was in danger.

Toto knows he must hide quickly.

19

Honey makes sure the baboons have gone before she goes to Toto.

The baboons stopped, and ate some fresh green leaves. Then very slowly, they moved away. Toto was safe! Honey waited until the baboons were out of sight. Then she went to Toto's hiding place in the grass and licked his face.

But it was not long before
Toto was in new danger.

Honey and Toto leave home

One morning, just as the sun had risen, we went out to watch Honey and Toto as usual. We could not find them anywhere. Then we found out that three male lions were prowling nearby. They would certainly kill Toto if they found him.

We began to feel worried.

Lions often kill cheetah cubs. They do not want them to grow up.

We saw the three lions go to the place where Honey and Toto usually slept during the night. They were looking for a **lioness**. But Honey and Toto had already gone. Honey knew that it was a dangerous place and so she had decided to leave.

We were not surprised that Honey had moved to a new home. It was too dangerous.

We saw Toto only one more time. Honey and Toto were sheltering from the rain on a rocky hillside.

24

The next day, Toto had disappeared.
We never found out what happened to him.
Perhaps a lion had killed him. We were very sad.

But Honey's story does not end here.

Honey's Boys

The following year, Honey had three new cubs, and we called them Honey's Boys. They were gorgeous and full of life – just like Toto.

They lived to grow up into strong and successful hunters.
We were lucky enough to watch them as they fought and played
and raced across that beautiful part of the African plains.

*Honey's Boys grew up
and hunted together.*

Cheetahs are endangered

For many years, the number of cheetahs in the wild has been dropping.

There are three reasons why is this happening.

The main reason is because cheetahs have to travel over many miles on the African plains in search of food. Today, people want to live on the plains, growing food, keeping animals and building houses. These developments are shrinking the cheetah's habitat. Because of the presence of more humans, there are fewer animals that cheetahs can hunt. Cheetahs need to find places to live where they are protected, like the big game parks. But even in the parks, cheetahs are not always safe from humans, because **poachers** steal cheetah cubs. They sell the cubs in other countries as pets and many cubs die.

CONSERVATION FUND UK
www.cheetah.org.uk

The Cheetah Conservation Fund UK (CCF UK) is the UK affiliate of CCF, a global leader in the research and conservation of the cheetah, with HQs in Namibia. CCF runs award-winning programmes in education, conservation and habitat restoration and is dedicated to protecting the cheetah in the wild. CCF UK supports CCF by raising awareness of the plight of the cheetah and funds to support the work of CCF in Namibia and throughout Africa.

Cheetahs are also at risk from other animals. They can run faster than any other creature on Earth, but they are not strong. They do not defend their kills, especially from other big cats, like lions or leopards. If they are injured in a fight, they cannot hunt for food.

Cheetah cubs are **at risk**. This is because they grow up on the grassland, where they are often killed by other animals. Fewer and fewer cubs are growing up to reach adulthood.

The wild places where cheetahs live must be kept safe. People can help by reducing their impact on the cheetah's natural habitat. Then cheetahs will be able to wander over the African plains, as they have always done.

Glossary

at risk	in danger
courage	bravery
exploring	going round a place to see what is there
hyenas	wild animals that look like dogs, hunt in groups and make noises like a human laugh
lioness	female lion
mound	small hill
plains	large area of flat land
poachers	people who hunt or steal animals illegally
prey	animal that is hunted and killed by another animal
triumph	important success
whined	made a long, high, sad sound

Index

Honey and Toto: the story of a cheetah family Jonathan and Angela Scott

Teaching notes written by Sue Bodman and Glen Franklin

Using this book

Content/theme/subject

This beautiful book features stunning real-life photography from the work of Jonathan and Angela Scott. The text is built around the pictures to tell the life of a young cheetah cub, Toto, and his mother, Honey, on the plains of the Masai Mara, in Kenya, Africa. Written in part as a recount, the Scotts tell their story directly to the reader, whilst additional information about cheetahs is provided through a variety of non-fiction features.

Language structure

- Clear examples of the structures appropriate to the genre are provided, such as the use of personal voice: *'We called the mother cheetah 'Honey'* (p.2) and present tense, generic report style: *'Cheetahs can run at 70 miles per hour'* (p.5).
- Captions are written in the present tense (for example: *'Toto knows he must hide quickly.'* on p. 19), engaging the reading in the action.

Book structure/visual features

- Purpose and audience is clearly supported by text organisation and layout.
- There is a variety of appropriate non-fiction layout features employed.

Vocabulary and comprehension

- Subject-specific vocabulary relates to the topic and content of the book.
- Longer, multisyllabic words provide opportunity to rehearse word-reading skills.

Curriculum links

Science – Use information texts and the Internet to find out more about cheetahs.

Literacy – Research other wild-life writers who have chronicled their life with animals. Look at the writing style used in recounting their experiences.

Learning outcomes

Children can:

- recognise the writing styles used in different text types, commenting on the effectiveness in conveying the author's message
- comment on the how different purposes are reflected in more complex non-fiction texts
- read with accuracy and demonstrate understanding by responding to questions.

Planning for guided reading

Lesson One: Writing style and purpose

Begin by establishing the type of book: *The title is 'Honey and Toto: The story of a cheetah family'. Do you think this is going to be a story book? Why not?'* Discuss how this is a true story, told as a recount, and identify why it is a non-fiction book (picking up on familiar features of information texts such as an index and glossary, and the use of fact boxes and maps).

Turn to p.2. and ask the children to read this page quietly to themselves. Share what they have found out about Jonathan and Angela Scott. Look at p.3 and consider the line: *'It is a story of the triumph of courage.'* Check the definition of the two glossary words, and consider what the authors meant by this.

On p.4, look at the writing conventions that show the authors are narrating the events (the use of *'we'*, and a more informal style of language that addresses the reader directly: *'So, like all cheetahs, Honey was used to danger.'*) Compare with the more formal language structures used in the fact box and caption on p.5, and consider the difference in purpose here (to inform the reader). You may wish to remind the children about the distinct purposes of labels and captions: the label on p.4 is describing what is happening in the picture. It is not providing additional information. It is not a complete sentence and therefore has no punctuation. Look also at the map on p.4, perhaps finding Kenya on a world map or globe and seeing where it is in relation to your children's own region.